Muslim Scientists

IBN KHALDUN
The Great Historian

Published by Ali Gator Productions
Copyright © 2021 Ali Gator Productions, Second Edition,
First Published 2019

National Library of Australia Cataloguing–in–Publication (CIP) data:
Ahmed Imam
ISBN: 978-1-921772-66-5
For primary school age, Juvenile fiction, Dewey Number: 823.92

Adapted from the original title Ilmuan Muslim Ibnu Khaldun first published by Pelangi Mizan.
Copyright © 2015 by Author Selly Astari and Risma Dewi, Illustrator Nano. Printed in Indonesia.

T: +61 (3) 9386 2771
P.O. Box 2536, Regent West, Melbourne Victoria, 3072 Australia
E: info@ali-gator.com **W:** www.ali-gator.com

بِسْمِ اللهِ الرَّحْمٰنِ الرَّحِيْمِ

BISMILLAHIR RAHMANIR RAHIM

IN THE NAME OF ALLAH, MOST GRACIOUS, MOST MERCIFUL

Inspiring our children to learn about
the great Muslim scientists, scholars
and adventurers from
the Golden Age of Islam.

NOTES TO PARENTS AND TEACHERS

The Muslim Scientists Series aims to introduce to young readers some of the famous Muslim scientists, scholars and adventurers who discovered and invented many things that we use today and take for granted.

It is our hope that young children will be inspired by these amazing people and be encouraged to pursue their own path of discovery and questioning. It all starts with a passion for learning.

Whilst reading about Ibn Khaldun, ˝The Great Historian˝, talk to the children about Andalusia, Islamic Spain. Do they know about the history of the Muslims in Spain ?

Why it is important as Muslims to know our history, world history and history from the Islamic world.

Discuss how Ibn Khaldun balanced his Islamic life with his political and legal roles and was successful in all areas.

In Sha Allah (God Willing) if this series helps to inspire our young readers to be the next generation of thinkers, to better mankind through inventions and discoveries, then we have truly met our goal.

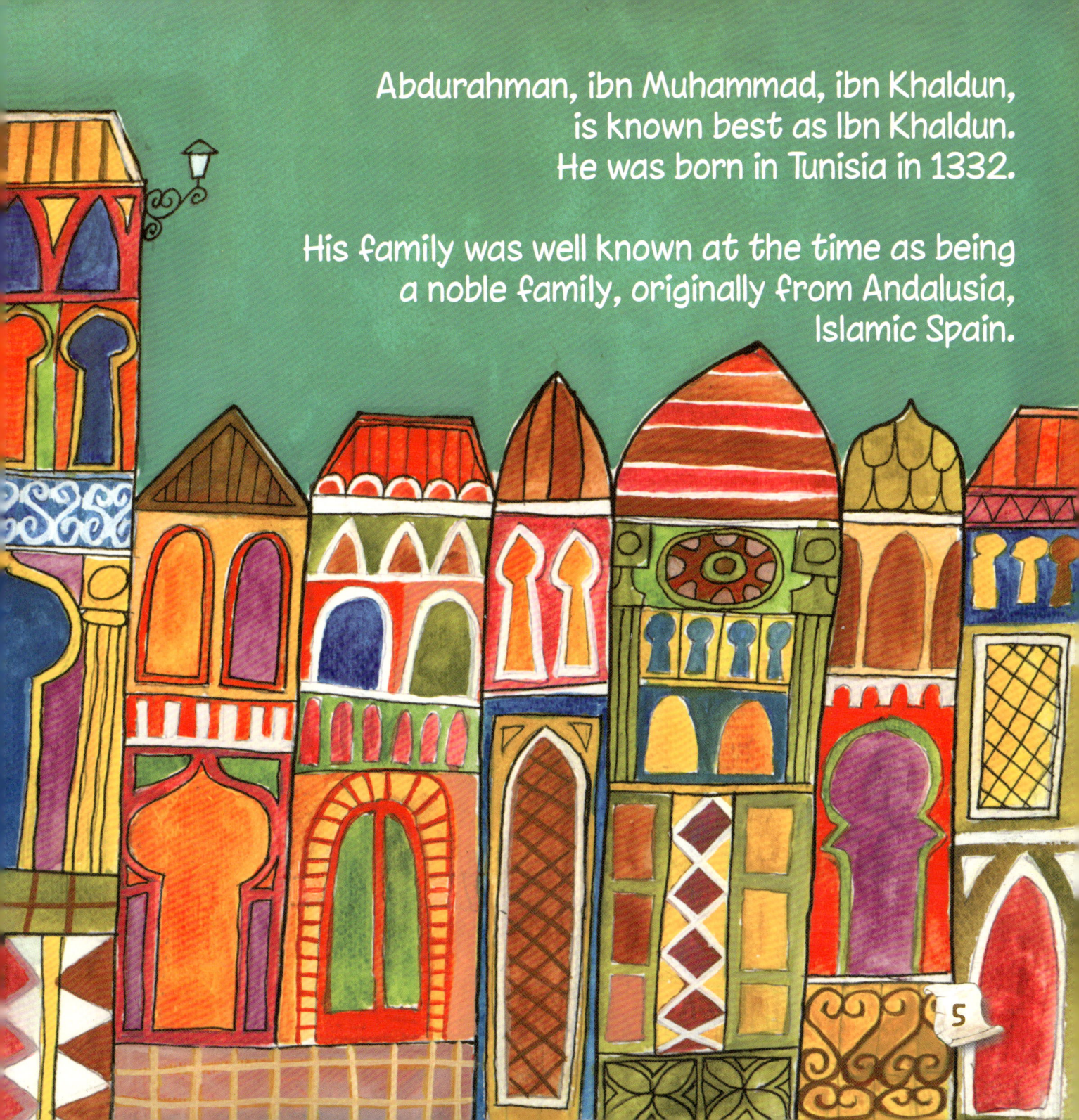

Abdurahman, ibn Muhammad, ibn Khaldun,
is known best as Ibn Khaldun.
He was born in Tunisia in 1332.

His family was well known at the time as being
a noble family, originally from Andalusia,
Islamic Spain.

6

Ibn Khaldun's father was a scientist, who taught him many things, including mathematics, logic and philosophy.

Ibn Khaldun was also a great student of Islam, and memorized the whole Qur'an fully by heart.

Ibn Khaldun started in a political career and worked for the ruler of Tunisia, and soon became a minister in the government.

8

When given the opportunity to move to Egypt, he did and became a professor at a famous college and was appointed a Supreme Judge.

During his life Ibn Khaldun developed a passion for history.

He studied and researched at every opportunity.

His knowledge on the subject grew so much that
he wanted to share it with everyone around him.

Ibn Khaldun wanted to write a history of the world.

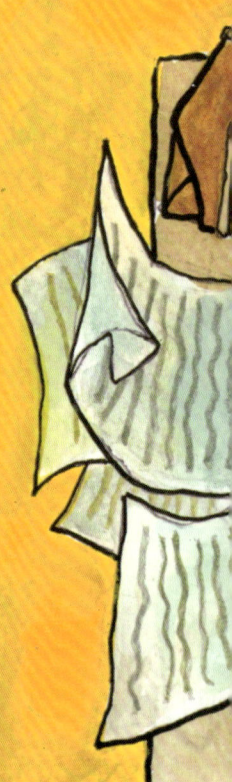

After many years Ibn Khaldun wrote his famous book, Kitabul 'Ibar or "Book of Lessons" which was actually seven books.

It is considered a document covering universal history.

The most famous one is titled "Muqaddimah", the introduction.

For centuries anyone who wanted to study history, social sciences, politics or economics at university would use Ibn Khaldun's "Muqaddimah" as their main source.

17

From this book, Ibn Khaldun became famous throughout the world and became known as a great historian, social scientist, and political expert.

19

As a great student and teacher, Ibn Khaldun had developed a very large library of books.

He would write with a quill and parchment.

Can you see these in his library ?

21

Ibn Khaldun's books were translated into many languages.

So now the whole world knows
about Ibn Khaldun.

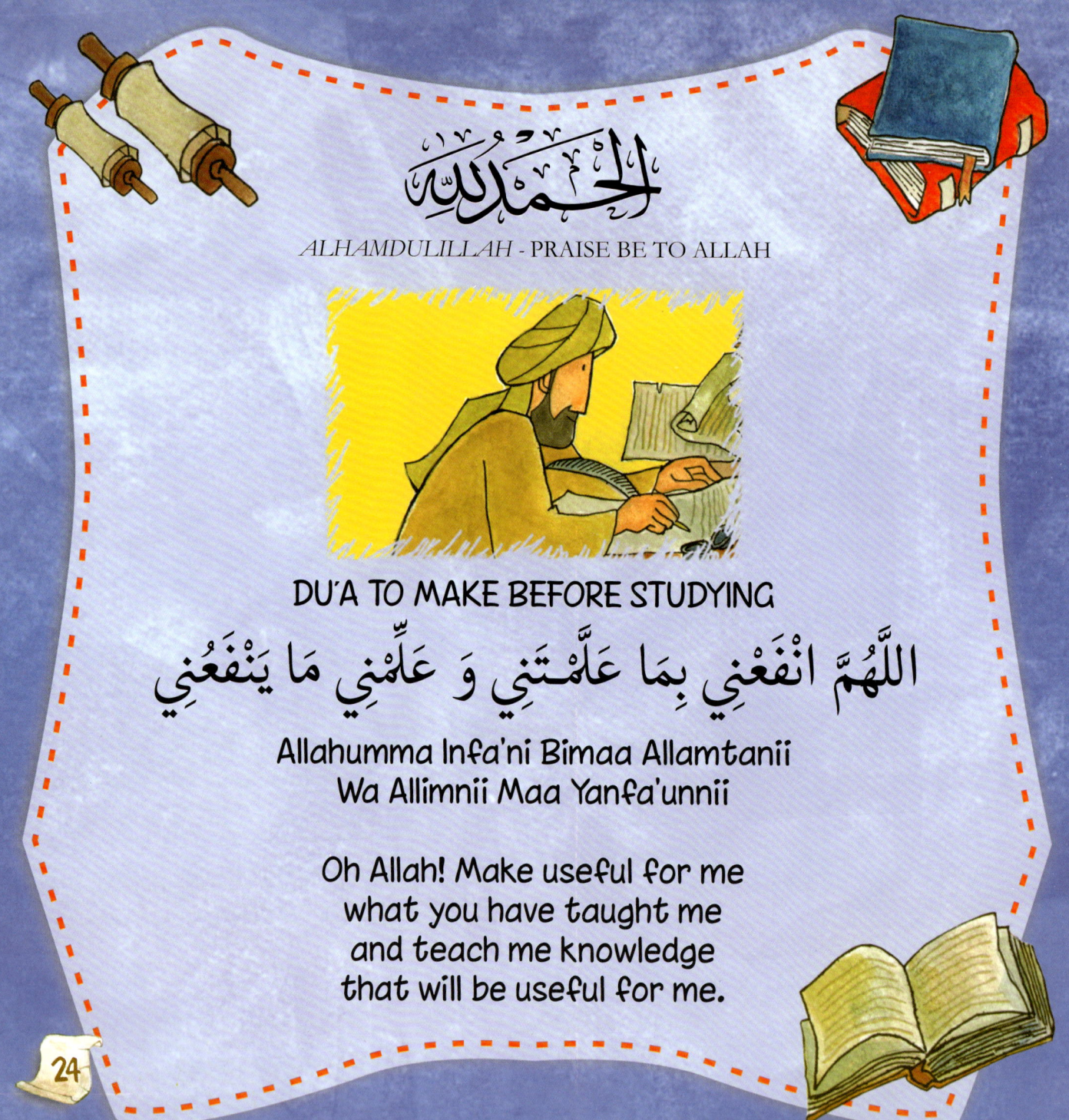

الْحَمْدُ لِلَّهِ

ALHAMDULILLAH - PRAISE BE TO ALLAH

DU'A TO MAKE BEFORE STUDYING

اللَّهُمَّ انْفَعْنِي بِمَا عَلَّمْتَنِي وَ عَلِّمْنِي مَا يَنْفَعُنِي

Allahumma Infa'ni Bimaa Allamtanii
Wa Allimnii Maa Yanfa'unnii

Oh Allah! Make useful for me
what you have taught me
and teach me knowledge
that will be useful for me.